S0-AWM-264

HIDDEN HEROINES
Women in American History

BOOKS BY ELAINE LANDAU

HIDDEN HEROINES: Women in American History

WOMAN, WOMAN! Feminism in America

BLACK IN AMERICA: A Fight for Freedom
(with Jesse Jackson)

DEATH: Everyone's Heritage

YOGA FOR YOU

PICTURE CREDITS

The Bettmann Archive, Inc.: pp. 33, 55, 57, 80
Culver Pictures, Inc.: p. 64
Denver Public Library, Western History Department: p. 52
International Ladies Garment Workers Union: p. 88
Library of Congress: pp. 9, 16, 34, 35, 42, 43, 45, 48, 49, 62, 71, 73, 76
Montana Historical Society, Bertie Lord Collection: p. 58
Nebraska State Historical Society: p. 53
New York Public Library Picture Collection: pp. 17, 20, 23, 69, 87
New York Public Library Rare Books Division: p. 6
Vassar College: p. 79

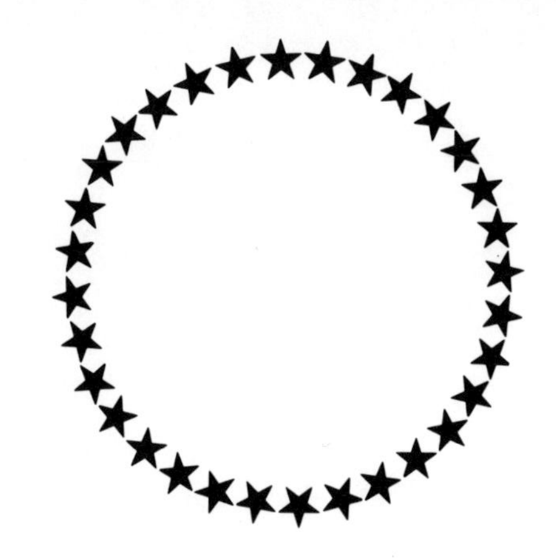

HIDDEN HEROINES
Women in American History

By ELAINE LANDAU

Illustrated with photographs and engravings

JULIAN MESSNER

NEW YORK

Published by Julian Messner, a Simon & Schuster Division of Gulf & Western Corporation. Simon & Schuster Building, 1230 Avenue of the Americas, New York, N.Y. 10020.

Printed in the United States of America
Design by Marjorie Zaum

Third Printing, 1978

For my Mother

Library of Congress Cataloging in Publication Data
Landau, Elaine.
Hidden heroines: women in American history.
SUMMARY: Discusses the role of women in the United States as they helped to build the colonies, settle the frontier, and defend their country and then struggled to possess the fundamental rights of citizens.
1. Women—United States—History—Juvenile literature. [1. Women—History] I. Title.
HQ1410.L25 301.41'2'0973 75-23068
ISBN 0-671-32747-X MCE

Contents

Signs and pamphlets describing a glorious New World encouraged English women and men to journey across the Atlantic.

NOVA BRITANNIA.

OFFERING MOST

Excellent fruites by Planting in

VIRGINIA.

Exciting all ſuch as be well affected

to further the ſame.

LONDON

Printed for SAMVEL MACHAM, and are to be ſold at

his Shop in Pauls Church-yard, at the

Signe of the Bul-head.

1609.

1

☆
☆
☆

Welcome to Paradise

☆

COME TO THE NEW WORLD
Any woman who journies over
Will think herself in Heaven!

SIGNS LIKE THESE, PAINTED IN GOLD LETTERS ON FINE white parchment, were to be seen almost everywhere in England during the early 1600s. They hung in taverns, fish and food markets, theaters, parks, bakery shops, and dress stores. Whenever a woman left her house, she would likely see an attractive New World notice. Or she would hear some favorable talk about the distant land.

The advertisements were put up by British companies trying to establish colonies in America. Having their own colonies across the sea would give the British an additional market for their goods. The merchants also wanted the raw materials the colonies could sell to them. The thick forests would produce enough timber to build a large English fleet, and the animal furs could be made into warm clothing, bedding, and rugs.

At first the companies believed that only men were needed to develop the land. They soon realized they were wrong. Sailors or wealthy adventurers usually stayed in the New World only a few months. When the thrill of exploring wore away, the men hurried back to England.

Even settlements established by men who intended to stay rarely succeeded. Many men returned home because they missed their families. Those who remained often left their settlements to explore, or to trap animals for their fur or to find gold.

Small groups of Spanish, French, Dutch, Swedish, and German settlers had also tried to establish New World colonies, but most colonists were English.

It was clear that something needed to be done if the English colonies were to grow. As one trading company official wrote:

> If the good land is to grow to strength, we must plant with both women and men. Such strength is needed. Families must spread into generations, so our colonies will never be pierced without.

Now the merchants began to look for women colonists! They hoped women who went with their husbands to the New World would keep the men from deserting. Besides, hard working women could supply much of the labor needed to build a colony.

Like the men who settled in the New World, the women came for many reasons. Some wanted adventure; some came to earn a better living; some wanted the religious freedom that they did not have in their homeland.

The companies welcomed any woman willing to go to America, regardless of why she came. Women who expressed even the least interest were told of warm,

Some of the women arriving in Jamestown came to marry male settlers. Colonial women usually married at an early age. Many brides were only thirteen or fourteen years old.

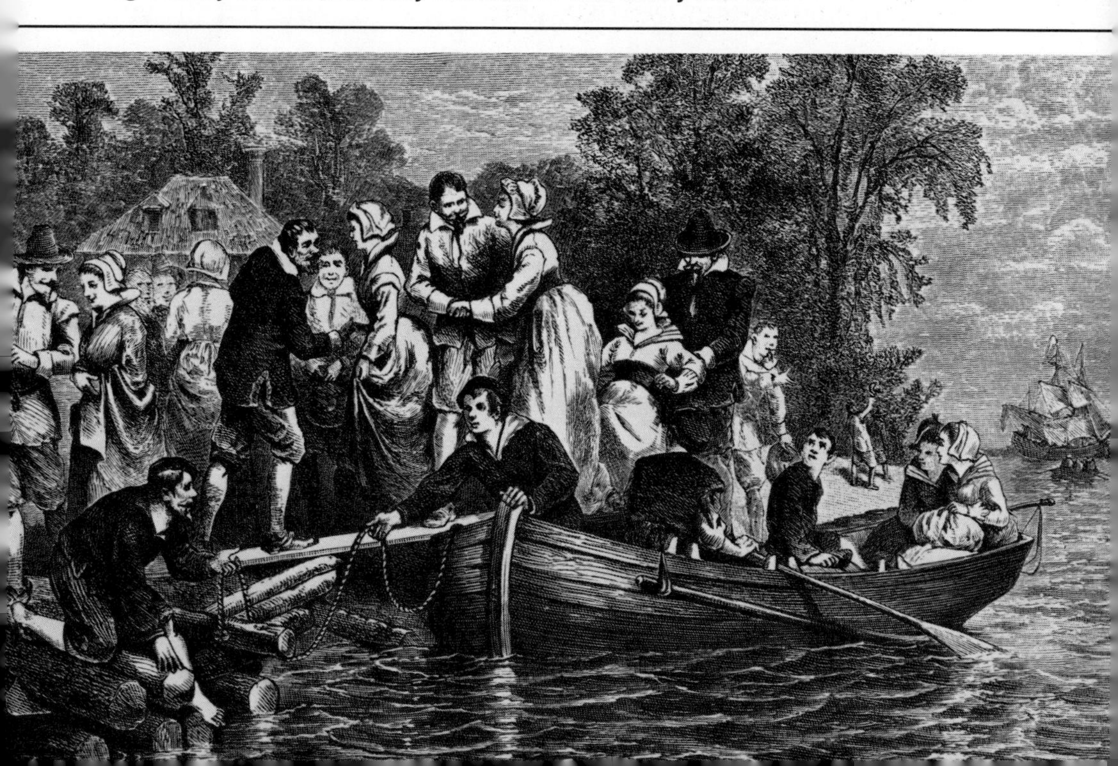

balmy summer months, of pleasant walks through sweet-smelling fields while listening to singing birds, and of picking pretty flowers and wild strawberries four times bigger than any in England. They were not told much about the hard work and harsh winters in this strange land.

As a result, twenty women and children were aboard the English ship *Blessing* when it arrived at the Jamestown colony, in Virginia, in August of 1609.

However, the English did not find colonization very easy. Two other British settlements in Virginia had failed before Jamestown was settled. Everyone hoped the families would make a difference. But the women soon found they were not blessed with the "Heaven" they heard about.

The Jamestown colony had been founded on a low-lying peninsula in the James River near a large malaria-breeding swamp. At first, only a few colonists fell ill with malaria. But soon the fever spread.

And as an early and cold winter set in, the colony was faced with starvation. The small ships of colonial times had barely enough food and supplies for the passengers and crew on long voyages. And, they also had to carry enough supplies for the return voyage. So, extra food could not be brought from the homeland.

The colonists depended on what little corn they were able to grow, or they borrowed from their Indian neighbors.

At first, the Indians gave freely to the colonists. They brought them corn from their fields and fowl they had hunted in the forests. Indian women taught the English women how to prepare the corn and how to make stone and wood tools for cleaning the fowl.

But a few colonists wanted even more corn than the Indians gave them. So they began to steal from the Indians, who were already short in their supply of corn. Some settlers even burned down Indian homes to get control of their fields. Angered by these evil actions, the Indians withdrew their food and friendship. Now the colonists had to worry about both starvation and Indian attacks.

However, Jamestown's troubles were to get worse. The colonists found that most of the small supply of corn they had stored had been eaten by rats. What was left had rotted from exposure. And, fearful of Indian attacks, the settlers stayed out of the forests where they might have hunted or trapped animals to eat.

As a result, the colonists nearly starved to death during the winter of 1609-10. Everyone suffered, including the Grant family. Elizabeth and Matthew Grant and their daughter JoAnna had come to the New World in high spirits. They had heard that anyone willing to work hard would do well in the new land.

The Grants were almost penniless the day they arrived in Jamestown. The only thing of value that they owned was a small gold music box, left to Elizabeth by her grandmother. And during the voyage to America, Elizabeth learned that she was to have a second child.

Although there would be another mouth to feed, Elizabeth Grant was glad both her children would be able to grow up in the New World. Besides, in a few years, the child would be old enough to help with the farmwork.

But Matthew Grant was among those sick with malaria, and Elizabeth put aside all her plans for her family's future. Their survival became her only concern. She cared for Matthew, provided food, and patched the battered cabin that sheltered them. But winter set in, and famine—and the weakened Matthew died.

Elizabeth, now in her seventh month of pregnancy, had to dig her husband's grave alone. She said what she knew of the religious service. The colony's clergyman had been one of the first to die during the famine.

Now Elizabeth and the other Jamestown women faced the almost impossible task of providing meals for their families. At first they killed all the horses and dogs. Often they tried to do so in secret to spare their children the knowledge of what they ate.

When this source of food gave out, the women found other animals. Rising before dawn, they ran out on the snow-covered fields and lay on their stomachs with their ears to the frozen ground. They remained there silent, without moving a muscle, anxiously listening for the sound of a snake or a mouse they might catch for food.

Elizabeth and JoAnna dug through the snow with their bare hands to search for dead herbs and weeds they could eat. The bitter cold made the hunger even harder to bear. To keep warm, Elizabeth tore away bits of their cabin to use for firewood.

But all Elizabeth's efforts did little good. She watched JoAnna grow thinner and paler, and die in midwinter. Elizabeth was exhausted from hunger and grief. She thought if she could only live long enough to have the baby, another woman might care for the child until it grew older.

Each day Elizabeth walked from cabin to cabin begging her neighbors for food. But they, too, were starving. Then one day, almost directly in front of her cabin, she spied two men who were about to eat a large rat they had just killed.

Elizabeth pleaded with the men for a piece. They refused. In desperation, she ran into her cabin to get the small gold music box her family had cherished. She offered it to the men for a bite of the rat. But gold no longer meant anything to settlers who had to struggle with Jamestown's cold and famine. The men sent her away.

Two days later, Elizabeth Grant was found lying dead in the snow. She had starved to death.

Though the Grant family did not survive, other settlers came to the New World to take their place. And although many of them endured hardships, few suffered as did the early Jamestown settlers.

2

☆
☆
☆

Heroic Housewives

☆

Over the next hundred years, English colonists continued to set up farms and towns all along the Atlantic seaboard. As late as 1738, some colonies still advertised for "honest members of the female sex who would not regret to marry in the New World and establish an orderly household."

There were usually many more males than females in the colonies. Men outnumbered women three-to-one in New England, while there were six men for every woman in Virginia. So women had their choice of marriage partners. Many were independent enough to do their own proposing.

One such woman was Betsy Hansford of Virginia. It was the custom in Betsy's colony that a rejected suitor could ask a member of the clergy to help him talk the woman of his choice into marrying him. After Betsy refused to wed a young Virginia man, he went directly to Reverend John Camm. Reverend Camm, the parish rector, had baptized Betsy, and often advised her on important matters.

The Reverend began calling on Betsy several times a week. He continually quoted from the Bible to convince her of the blessings of marriage, and urged her to accept the young man. Several months passed, but Betsy still refused.

By this time, the Reverend was ready to admit defeat. One evening, he told Betsy he would stop calling on her. But, Betsy insisted that he continue to visit. She explained that he could learn in the Bible why she rejected the young man.

When Reverend Camm returned home that evening, he opened his Bible to the page and lines Betsy had told him to read. To his amazement the words that greeted his eyes read "...thou art the man." At last he understood why Betsy Hansford had been so firm in her decision. She had wanted to marry the Reverend all along.

Reverend Camm was pleased by Betsy's boldness. He soon returned her feelings, and the two were married within the year.

Once married, most colonial women became housewives who spent much of their time caring for their families and homes. A colonial mother was expected to have many children, often as many as ten to fifteen. It was generally considered patriotic to have large families,

Some women became mothers at the age of fifteen, and a few were grandmothers at thirty. Baptisms were joyous events. But even though a great number of children were born, many died in infancy.

to make the colonies stronger. Besides, parents wanted children to help with the work and care for them in their old age.

Mothers were entirely responsible for child care. Their other duties varied according to the amount of money the family had.

Housewives with less money usually worked an eighteen-hour day. Using remarkable skill and energy, they made almost everything their families needed.

They spun their own cotton and flax, and sewed the

warm clothing and quilts needed during the cold winters. They built their own spinning wheels with wood from small trees they chopped down in the forests and hauled back to their homes.

The country housewife cared for the family's barnyard animals. She milked the cow and made butter from its milk. She plowed the earth, planted vegetable seeds, and took care of the growing plants. She made all the beer and cider her family drank. And, of course, she did all the cooking. Pork was a popular main dish because it was so easy to find. Large numbers of wild hogs roamed about the wooded areas, fattening themselves on roots and

Three generations of colonial women make clothing for winter. The grandmother cards the flax, the mother spins it, and the daughter boils the dye.

nuts. To have a fine roast pork dinner, one needed only to catch a hog, and colonial women soon became experts at this.

By the time the children turned six, they were expected to help their parents. The boys worked with their fathers to build the cabins and furniture as well as do most of the farming and hunting. The girls remained with their mothers doing "women's work," which meant caring for their homes and families.

However, when the men needed help, women and girls did jobs usually considered too difficult for them. Often they pulled plows, killed deer, and chopped down large trees. But no matter how exhausted their women became, no colonial man ever sat behind a spinning wheel!

However, some women led more pleasurable lives. They were the wives and daughters of successful tobacco planters.

The colonists had learned from the Indians that smoking tobacco could be enjoyable. They began to grow their own tobacco, and export some of their crops to England. The English, who quickly became fond of smoking, demanded more and more tobacco from the colonies. By 1638, Virginia exported over 1,400,000 pounds of tobacco yearly.

Soon, smoking became popular all over Europe. Other countries were eager for New World tobacco. Colonial planters cultivated more of it. Now large fields of tobacco were growing in the Maryland and North Carolina colonies, as well as in Virginia.

Planters who lived near deep waterways or harbors could ship their crops directly to Europe. They traded their tobacco for manufactured goods to make their families more comfortable.

While most of the backwoods farmers and poorer colonists still lived in crude green-timber houses or cabins, many tobacco planters had stylish wood or brick homes. Several very rich planters built big waterfront homes surrounded by beautiful grounds.

The main duties of a wealthy housewife in the southern colonies centered around providing meals for her family and being hostess to a large number of guests. Friends were invited to eat at their homes each night and travelers in need of lodging were always welcomed. The wife of a rich colonist planned the menus and made certain the food was properly served. To delight her guests' appetites, she made sure that a wide variety of delicious dishes were prepared.

Dinner usually consisted of several courses, all of which were set down on the table at once. A typical dinner might begin with *salmagundy,* a cold dish of sliced chicken, veal, turkey, eggs, and fresh fish, attractively arranged on a bed of lettuce. Next, a guest could try any of the different dinner meats, broiled, roasted, or fried, and served with rich stuffings and gravies. A variety of fowl and fish platters were also served, as were delicious meat pies. To complement the meat and fowl, the hostess served carrots, beets, asparagus, squash, and several kinds of potatoes. The table was also piled high with salads, freshly baked loaves of bread, butter, milk, and cheese.

Dessert would probably include a large *tangy,* a very popular colonial pudding—made of two quarts of rich white cream, twenty-five eggs, a pound of finely-ground nuts and topped with sugared orange slices. Guests

Large plantations, with smokehouse, dairy, mill, and other operations run by women, were small communities in themselves.

would finish their evening meal with drinks of rum, brandy, tea, or hot chocolate.

The vegetables the housewife served were grown in her own garden, the fish and meats cured in her smokehouse, the chicken kept in her poultry yard, and the butter, cream, eggs, and milk brought in from her dairy. She managed all these operations, which were scattered about the estate. Whatever wasn't produced in the colonies, she imported from England.

Running a large estate was like running a big business. One rich colonial housewife reported that in a year her family and guests had eaten 27,000 pounds of pork, 550 bushels of wheat, and 150 gallons of rum. Over 100 pounds of flour were used weekly.

The busy hostess also had to make sure the rooms were cleaned and stocked with fresh towels and linens, as many guests stayed overnight or for several days. For entertainment, they held dances and gave concerts. The housewives tried to be aware of the needs of their guests at all times. This meant that many nights they slept for only one or two hours. Often they did all of these many tasks while raising large families of their own.

These remarkable colonial women were actually America's first hotel managers!

3

☆
☆
☆

They Ran Ferries, Farms, and Inns

☆

NOT ALL COLONIAL WOMEN WERE HOUSEWIVES. SOME women chose not to marry, while others were forced to look for new ways of living when their husbands died.

At times planters' widows who inherited large houses turned them into inns for the use of travelers. Their past experience in running large households and entertaining many guests proved to be very valuable in the new businesses. The women stocked their cellars with the finest wines and liquors, and served their patrons tempting meals. And they hired singers and musicians to entertain nightly.

Many women placed advertisements for their inns in local newspapers. Some ads promised to provide "Good Stabling for Horses and Lodgings for their Grooms". Others offered "the best Liquors and Relishes."

The countryside was dotted with rivers, lakes, and

streams. To get across, travelers had to use ferries operated by women innkeepers. Even where there were no inns, women often ran the ferries.

In 1657, a Mrs. Fenwich was granted 500 pounds of tobacco by the Maryland Assembly for "her trouble in entertaining and setting people across the river." Appointed by the North Carolina Council in 1715, Anne Wilson ran "a good and sufficient ferry" over a river which connected her plantation to the next. The council declared that no one else could "presume to ferry over any horse or person within at least five miles either above or below that place."

J. H. & [illegible]

Coach Makers,

R[illegible] inform the public that they continue [illegible] on the Coach-making business, in all [illegible] branches. They [illegible] a great variety of [illegible] GIGS and CHAISES, of every description, which they offer to the public on the most liberal terms, for cash or approved credit. Those who wish to purchase are requested to call and examine their work and materials.

An active LAD, [illegible] the age of fifteen, will find good encouragement at the above business.

May 15. 61

STEAM-BOAT HOTEL,

Water Street, New Haven.

MRS. A. BABCOCK,

HAS removed her establishment from the New-England Coffee-House, in Church-St. New-Haven, to that large and commodious house in Water-Street, near Tomlinson's Bridge, formerly owned and occupied by Mr. Platt. This house, being located near the place where the Steam-Boat FULTON arrives, affords to Gentlemen and Ladies, who may be traveling to and from New-York, conveniences equal to other public houses in this city. Every attention will be paid to her guests to render their stay agreeable. The best of liquors [illegible] constantly on hand.

She returns her thanks to those who encouraged her former establishment, and will spare no pains to merit a [illegible] of her present one.

Gentlemen and Ladies who may visit the sea shore for their health, can be accommodated in no better situation than here, [illegible] directly fronts the Sound, in view of all vessels passing and repassing, and during the summer season is delightfully situated to receive refreshing breezes from the sea.

June 12. tf 85

WAGGONS,

ON AN IMPROVED PLAN.

THE objection to waggons as a pleasant carriage, has been [illegible] the want of an easy motion, the difficulty of getting in and [illegible] ing—Those who are in want of [illegible] of the above description, will find [illegible] difficulties which attend waggons, obviated, by calling at the shop of the subscriber—The principle on which Waggons can be built, is much lighter than those of other carriages; they can be built in a handsome style, for one or two horses, at much less expence; besides the consideration that it does not cost so much to keep them in repair.—Other Carriages made as usual, and all Repairing done on the shortest notice.

N. B. All orders thankfully received and punctually attended to, by the public's humble servant,

JAMES BREWSTER.

Elm-st. North of the Colleges, }
Dec. 12, 1814. } tf 59

WAGGONS FOR SALE.

THE subscriber has on hand, and now finishing, at the new building directly opposite the public Well, in Broadway, a great variety of one and two-horse WAGONS, which are warranted to be finished as substantial and neat as any others which can be purchased elsewhere, and are offered for sale at a reasonable price.

ALSO, FOR SALE,

A variety of HARNESSES

Several second hand Chaises and Waggons.

JAMES HEADLEY, Jun.

N. B. Cash paid for White Oak Spokes, Ash and Oak Plank.

New-Haven, June 12. 85

STEAM-BOAT FULTON.

For the better accommodation of the public, the proprietors of the Steam-Boat FULTON, have determined to run her six times a week between New-York and New-Haven. This new arrangement commenced on Monday, the 12th inst. The days of starting are as follows, viz:—From New-York every Monday, Wednesday and Friday morning. From New-Haven every Tuesday, Thursday and Saturday morning.

June 20. 88

WAGGON TO LET.

A GENTEEL one horse Waggon to let, by

D. S. GLADDING.

Chapel-Street, June 19. 86

WANTED,

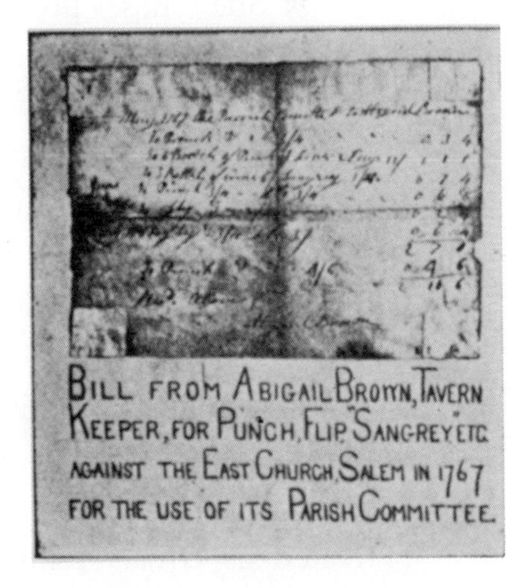

Colonial inns operated by women were gathering places for townspeople and travelers. Lodge meetings, public balls, lottery drawings, cockfights, and even duels were held there.

Not all women who inherited plantations turned their mansions into inns. Some preferred to carry on their husbands' businesses.

These women were as capable as their husbands had been and sometimes even more so—as was Mary Willing Byrd. Mary's husband William had inherited a large fortune and an immense estate from his father. But William gambled and spent his money foolishly, so there was little left when he died.

His young widow took over the estate and family finances, and supported herself and her eight children. A neighbor wrote of her:

> She has preserved his beautiful house, situated on the James River and a large amount of personal property . . . Her care and activity have in some measure repaired the effects of her husband's dissipation, and her house is still the most celebrated, and the most agreeable of the neighborhood . . .

Other rich women plantation owners never married. Many single wealthy women had been attracted to the colonies because they had been promised they would be treated as equals with male colonists. Two such women, Mary and Margaret Brent, came to Maryland from from England with their brother. They claimed lands in their own names and established separate plantations.

Soon each sister owned over 1,000 acres of Maryland soil.

According to Maryland law, large land owners could act as judges to settle disputes among people in their area. Both Mary and Margaret Brent held their own courts. Margaret was able to make people pay what they owed her, and also helped other women collect what was owed them. It was often necessary to use the courts to collect debts, since men who borrowed money from women sometimes did not want to repay them.

Margaret Brent was so successful at her own business affairs that both women and men sought her advice. The Governor of Maryland appointed her to manage his estate in the event of his death.

Eliza Lucas was another colonial woman planter. At seventeen, she was left in charge of a large plantation in South Carolina when her father, a British officer, was stationed in the West Indies.

Eliza claimed to "love the vegetable world extremely," and she often tried experiments with growing plants. Her father sent her a variety of new seeds and plants, and Eliza soon discovered which crops grew best in South Carolina soil. She became very successful at growing cotton, West Indian corn, and ginger.

Once she wrote a friend, "I have planted a large fig orchard with design to dry and export them." In a later letter she added that she was quite busy "making a large plantation of oaks." She reasoned that such a crop would be very profitable "when oaks are more valuable then they are now, which you know will come when we are ready to build fleets."

But it was indigo that benefited Eliza Lucas and the South Carolina colony most. Indigo is a violet-blue dye obtained from the indigo plant, and it has always been in great demand.

After several experiments, Eliza Lucas succeeded in growing a perfect crop of indigo plants. To help her neighbors, she used one year's crop for seeds, and gave them to her neighbors without charge.

Eliza received many proposals of marriage during the time she ran the plantation and conducted her indigo experiments. However, she turned them all down. Often she stated that "a Single life is my only Choice."

Her father believed every woman should marry as soon as possible. He wrote several letters to his daughter encouraging her to marry the man he had chosen for her. In reply, Eliza wrote:

> Honored Sir:
>
> You propose Mr. L to me, but I am sorry I cannot have sentiments favorable enough of him to think on the subject. . . . Let him know that the riches of Chili and Peru put together if he had them, could not purchase sufficient esteem for him to make him my husband.
>
> And dear father, as I am but eighteen,

I hope you will put aside these thoughts of my marrying yet these two or three years at least.

Your most delightful and affectionate daughter,

Eliza Lucas

Much later, Eliza decided to marry. She chose Charles Pinckney, a man to whom she proposed herself. Eliza gave birth to two sons, Thomas and Charles, both of whom later became famous soldiers and statesmen. She raised her children while continuing to manage her estate and conduct farming experiments. Even in her old age, she was often referred to as the most active businesswoman in South Carolina.

4

☆
☆
☆

Making America Prosper

☆

AS TIME PASSED, THE ENGLISH SETTLEMENTS GREW. Thriving towns and villages sprang up. To help these new areas develop, women provided a variety of services.

Some became teachers. Colonial America did not have public school such as we have today. Parents either taught their children or paid someone to do it for them. Most colonial parents were very busy, and they only had time to teach their own trade to their children. But a good teacher could help her students learn many subjects.

Well-to-do colonists hired women called governesses to educate their children. A colonial governess lived in her employer's home. She taught reading, writing, arithmetic, music, and manners. In addition, she instructed the young girls in embroidery, needlework, and household budgeting.

Some governesses spoke several languages. Since such ability was highly thought of, these women could easily find work. One governess placed this advertisement in a small colonial newspaper, and received fifty offers of employment in two days!

> A young lady well acquainted with the French language—having resided for several years in France—wishes a place in a genteel family to instruct young ladies in French and other useful ornamental work.

Colonists who could not afford to hire a governess, sometimes put their children in schools run by unmarried women. These schools varied in size as well as in quality.

Some women simply took young girls into their homes for a few years to teach them to read and sew. But these girls spent very little of their time studying. They practiced reading for perhaps an hour, and spent the rest of the day learning to care for a home by helping their teacher clean her house.

In the evening, the teacher read passages from the Bible, as the students sat in a circle on the floor in front of the fireplace. To make sure they were paying attention, every once in a while she stopped her reading to question them about the text.

Other schools offered more varied studies. A number of women set up boarding schools for both girls and boys. The children lived at these schools throughout the year. In addition to learning to read and write, students were taught carpentry, tailoring, embroidery, music, painting, drawing, dancing, and social manners.

Some women contributed in other ways. They became doctors, and practiced "physick" and "chirgery"—as the practice of medicine was then called.

During colonial times, a doctor did not have to earn a medical degree. Anyone with a knowledge of what to do for illness or injury could become a doctor. Women were considered as able as men to heal—if not more so. As children, many of them had watched their mothers and grandmothers treat ill family and neighbors. Now, as adults, they used the same cures to become doctors.

These women were kept very busy. They could be called at any hour of the day or night. Their families had to be able to take care of themselves, for a doctor might be gone for several days at a time.

Katherine Shewsberry was a well known doctor in Virginia. She was also a wife and the mother of eight children. Katherine always kept an extra wagon in back of the house, that could be hitched up at a moment's notice. The wagon was stocked with medical supplies, books, candles, blankets, and dried foods. Katherine often took along her oldest daughter Beth to help her and to learn. By the time Beth turned fifteen, she was able to treat patients by herself.

Katherine and Beth used drugs they had learned to prepare from Indian women. The colonists had few of the remedies that they had depended on in England. They turned to the Indians for help and, in times of peace, the Indians were glad to give the settlers their secrets. Many Indian women were experts at brewing various herbs and roots and combining them into pills and potions. Other women learned these cures as well. Some became pharmacists and sold their pills, syrups, potions, and salves to earn a living.

Women played an important role as nurses. Families hired nurses to care for those who were very ill. When smallpox or other diseases broke out, nurses often took care of patients in their own homes. By separating the sick, they unwittingly helped to stop diseases from spreading further.

Although women doctors, pharmacists, and nurses all made valuable contributions, midwives were considered the most essential to health care. Midwives, not doctors, delivered babies.

Most midwives learned their trade from experienced midwives. But some received special instruction in midwifery at famous medical schools in Europe before they came to the colonies. One woman advertised her services as a midwife by stating that she had "studied the art of midwifery at college regularly. And practiced it afterwards with great success. She would gladly produce certificates from her professors."

A midwife was an important person in her community. Besides her skill in delivering babies, she was frequently called into court to testify as an expert witness. She might be asked to confirm someone's age, since she was present at the birth, or to repeat something a mother screamed out during labor.

The death of a midwife usually drew a large funeral. Those whom she had brought into the world, as well as their families and friends, usually attended. When an especially well-known midwife died in South Carolina, her name and achievements were cited in the community's newspaper.

> Thursday last died, greatly lamented, aged 73 years, Mrs. Elizabeth Hunt, a practicing midwife of this province. It was said to appear by an account regularly kept by her, that she had been present at the birth of nearly 4,000 children.

Colonial women engaged in many other important occupations. They worked as shoemakers, gunsmiths, and blacksmiths, and ran their own stores.

Those who owned large general stores offered a wide range of goods. Imported items included olives, spices, teas, sugar, chocolate, and rum. They also sold milk, butter, flour, vinegar, fruits, vegetables, and packages of garden seeds. Some store owners became well

Twin sisters Carine and Nellie Blair ran a blacksmith shop in the colonies.

known for their homemade foods and drinks, such as plum pudding, pickled herrings, and red wines.

Other women started America's first bakeries. Using their own recipes, they made tasty apple tarts, almond puddings, rice cups, lemon and orange creams, white custards, and rich plum cakes with apricot icing.

A large number of women operated dry goods stores. Their stock depended on what their customers needed. They sold ink, ledgers, guns, pistols, canes, flutes, violins, silver toothpicks, tortoise shell toothpick cases, gold watches, snuff, and toys such as dolls and marbles.

Women who were good dressmakers often owned

Many of the women who owned millinery shops took great pride in their merchandise. They traveled to London to learn the newest styles and to buy fabrics for the fashions they made.

large clothing shops. They made hats, dresses, gowns, cloaks, and suits in various styles. One woman advertised that she "dressed young ladies' heads with delicate bonnets adorned with silver buttons and velvet flowers." Others prided themselves on "hoop-petticoats, painted fans, brocaded topcoats" or "colored silk gloves and satin shoes."

To help them make the clothing, they hired young girls as assistants. In exchange for room and board—they were not paid for their work—the girls learned to manage a store and make patterns of the latest fashions. After a time, many of them left to start their own businesses.

There were women in the newspaper business, too. Among them was Mary Katherine Goddard of Maryland. When her brother William, publisher of the *Baltimore*

(Maryland) *Journal,* went to England for a few months, Mary agreed to run the paper during his absence.

When William did not return after two years, Mary took full control of the business. She published the newspaper in her own name, and made changes to improve its quality and appearance. She used new styles of type and also decorated the front page with engravings drawn by colonial artists. Mary soon became known as "an ex-

Women became active in the printing and bookbinding trades. In fact, the first complete book printed in the colonies, THE BAY PSALM BOOK, was published by a woman, Elizabeth Glover of Cambridge, Massachusetts.

pert and excellent type selector." It was said that her newspaper was "second to none in the colonies." She also operated a printing press and a small bookstore. She even found time to serve as postmistress, delivering mail until a federal postal system was established.

By the beginning of the eighteenth century, women were working in just about every kind of business. They were no longer forced to make everything they and their families needed. Now they often depended on products made by other women. And as women continued to leave their homes to run businesses, "women's work" came to mean making America prosper.

5

☆
☆
☆

Freedom Fighters Who Were Not Free

☆

COLONIAL BUSINESSES MAY HAVE FLOURISHED, BUT BY 1760 all was not well in the colonies. The King of England knew that many of the New World settlers had become quite wealthy through their businesses and trades. He was determined that they contribute to the homeland's treasury.

And so the British government put a separate tax on almost every important item the colonists needed. A mother buying milk for her baby paid an extra sum to King George. So did each student in the colonies who purchased a pad of paper.

The colonists were outraged by the taxes. They argued that the British king should not have taxed them at all. They were not represented in the British Parliament, and had no one to speak up for their rights.

But King George and Parliament ignored their protests. They refused to lift the taxes. And to make sure the colonists continued to pay, British soldiers were sent to Boston, where the protests were strongest. The colonists were ordered to take the men into their own homes. They were even forced to provide them with free food and lodgings.

Bitter feelings spread throughout the thirteen colonies. At times, the anger broke into violence, and lives were lost on both sides. After 6 years of this, the colonists were certain their differences could never be settled peacefully. They decided to officially declare the colonies a separate and independent nation.

On July 4, 1776, the colonists issued the Declaration of Independence. The Declaration was drawn up by a committee of powerful men. Women were neither asked to help write it or sign it. Politics were reserved for men.

With the Declaration of Independence, the colonists severed all ties with Great Britain. But King George was not about to let his colonies go without a struggle. The colonists would have to fight for their freedom. And the efforts of both women and men were needed to win that fight.

Women were encouraged to take an active part in the war. Newspapers which formerly described women as "too wise to wrinkle their foreheads with politics," now urged them not to be "tame onlookers." Some of "the young ladies from the best families in North Carolina refused to court any gentleman who had not been in the military." Other women chose more active roles.

Many refused to buy British merchandise—they hoped to hurt Britain's economy and so lessen their ability to wage war. As one woman from Philadelphia wrote:

> I have removed every English import from the family dinner table. We have not drunk tea since last Christmas, and don't expect to again until we've won the war. This way do I throw in my mite to the public good.

Women banded together to form patriotic organizations such as the "Daughters of Liberty." The women spun cloth with which they made soldiers' uniforms. They collected lead and melted it down for bullets.

In Philadelphia, over 1600 women formed an organization to buy supplies for the military. They decided to collect gold to turn into cash. Going from door to door, they begged their neighbors to contribute any gold item in their household. They were given things like forks, serving spoons, earrings, pens, ashtrays, snuff boxes, and clocks.

The less well-to-do colonists gave whatever they could. One nearly penniless woman whose husband had been killed donated her thin gold wedding band. The other colonists tried to convince her that such self-sacrifice was unnecessary. But she threw the ring into the wooden collection box saying, "My husband gave his life for our freedom. Now it is my turn to help. I am giving my most precious remembrance of him."

The gold drive was a success. And similar organizations quickly sprang up in New Jersey, South Carolina, and Massachusetts.

During the Revolution, women established the first hospitals in the United States. They took care of the sick and wounded, cooked for the patients, did the laundry, and cleaned the wards. There was a shortage of nurses, so the women often worked throughout the day and well into the night. Sometimes this meant getting only one or two hours of sleep for two or three nights at a time.

Some nurses collapsed from exhaustion. Others, in hospitals near the front lines, were wounded or even killed by stray enemy bullets. Yet for all this work and sacrifice, they received little payment. In 1776, Nurse Alice Redman wrote this letter to the governor of Maryland:

> Dear Governor:
>
> I have now been a nurse at the war hospital for a little over a year. I have been diligent and careful in my office and therefore humbly beg for an increase in pay.
>
> I am only allowed two dollars a month and at present time there are sixteen men that I must cook for and take care of. I am obligated to be up day and night with some of the patients. None of the nurses have

been allowed so much as a little coffee or tea and we are often hungry as there isn't enough food. I hope you will take these circumstances into consideration.

In duty bound I will forever pray.

Alice Redman

P.S. Out of that two dollars a month I have to buy brooms and soap for the hospital.

While the men were off fighting, the women were left alone at home to carry on. Young daughters or women who had always been housewives learned to run large estates or become blacksmiths or shopkeepers in just a few days.

They also had their own battles to fight. British soldiers robbed them of their supplies and looted their houses. To protect themselves, many women learned to shoot guns, but even this did little good. One person against five or six armed soldiers didn't have much of a chance.

Late one night in August of 1777, a band of British soldiers broke into a house in South Carolina. The woman of the house was unarmed. She tried to fight the soldiers off with her fists. One soldier drew his gun to frighten her, but she jumped him to get hold of the weapon. The gun went off and the woman was hit.

The sound of the bullet woke her ten year-old daughter who had been sleeping upstairs. The girl ran out on the staircase in time to see her mother fall and die. Terrified, she fled to a neighbor's home for safety.

Her nearest neighbor happened to be Eliza Lucas Pinckney, the woman who had become famous conducting plant experiments. Eliza's husband had died some years back, and her two sons were off fighting. She was now 67 years old and at home alone with her youngest granddaughter.

When the frightened girl told her story, Eliza reassured her. "Don't fear. No harm will come to you now." But she suspected that the British soldiers would soon arrive at her own home. They usually robbed all the houses in an area when they believed the women were alone. Eliza went to the weapons cabinet, and armed herself and the two young girls with rifles. The girls protested that they didn't know how to shoot. But Eliza said, "The British don't know that."

During the American Revolution, Nancy Hart and many other women defended their homes against invading British soldiers.

To prevent British soldiers from getting her crops, Ms. Schuyler set fire to her corn fields.

The three waited together in the dark living room, clutching their rifles. When Eliza heard the soldiers force open the door, she quickly lit several candles. The British were greeted by the sight of a well lit room in which three women pointed rifles at them. "Get out of my home, or I'll kill you," Eliza said calmly. The soldiers quickly apologized and hurried out the door.

Colonial women were determined not to aid the enemy in any way. To safeguard their valuables, they buried them under the houses or even in the family graveyards. They burned their fields so the British could not get their crops.

Officially, women were not permitted to take part in the actual fighting. But that didn't keep them out of combat. Some women disguised themselves as men. Deborah Gannett tied back her hair, put on men's clothing, and enlisted in the Continental Army. Using the name Robert Shurtliff, she fought bravely for over a year and a half.

Married women with no children, who did not have to mind stores or large farms, often went with their soldier-husbands to the army camps. Their duties were supposedly limited to cooking and washing laundry. But when the soldiers were tired and weak, the women took their turns guarding the camp. They also helped defend the camp during surprise British attacks.

Some women even took part in major battles. Mary Ludwig McCauley was one of these. She had joined her husband at his army camp in New Jersey. On a sizzling summer morning when he left with his troops to fight the battle of Monmouth, Mary refused to remain at the campsite.

It was so hot that the men found it difficult to fight. They were soon exhausted. To refresh them, Mary carried pitchers of water from a nearby stream. Before the battle was over, they began calling her "Molly Pitcher."

But Mary didn't spend all the afternoon carrying water. By midday, the sun began taking a heavy toll on the soldiers. Mary's husband was among the men who

Mary Ludwig McCauley, who worked as a servant in Pennsylvania before her marriage, fired her husband's cannon after he collapsed at the Battle of Monmouth. Many years later, she was awarded forty dollars for her service.

collapsed from heat stroke. She dragged him to a shaded area, safe from enemy fire, and gave him more cool water. Then she returned to the battle, where she took her husband's place on the firing line for the rest of the fighting.

Other women also served. Sybil Ludington was just sixteen when she rode forty-four miles through the night to warn the colonial militia that the British were going to attack Danbury, Connecticut.

The fighting lasted for six years. Then in 1783, a peace treaty was finally signed with Britain. Women had done their part to achieve that peace—and at great cost. Many of them lost their lives, their families, and their possessions.

Yet the Declaration of Independence, the document on which their new nation was founded, decreed that "all men are created equal"—and made no mention of women.

6

☆
☆
☆

Westward Ho! The Women

☆

After the American Revolution, seaboard settlers gradually began to look westward. During the late 1700s and early 1800s, swarms of pioneers headed for the rich lands lying directly beyond the Appalachian Mountains.

Most of these pioneers travelled in wagons or carts pulled by a horse or mule. Those who could afford to, brought cows for milk as well as to haul belongings. Poorer settlers set off on foot, taking only what they could carry.

The vast wilderness made their journey difficult. The settlers hacked their way over steep, narrow mountain ridges, swam across icy streams, and travelled down swiftly moving rivers on rafts. Thousands reached the fertile farmlands of Kentucky, Tennessee, Ohio, and Illinois, where they established frontier settlements. And by 1830, the first big wave of western migration had pushed the frontier across the Mississippi River, into the grassy plains beyond. This area later became the states of Missouri, Iowa and Arkansas.

Meanwhile, explorers, missionaries, traders, and fur trappers journeyed into the South and Southwest. When they returned, they told of lush pastures and valleys lying past the Rocky Mountains, thousands of miles away. Their stories excited many who were eager to set out for new lands and new adventures. By the 1840s, more people began the long journey westward.

But the frontier really boomed in 1848 with exciting news that thrilled the nation and echoed around the globe. Gold had been discovered in California! Thousands of people from all over the world hurriedly flocked West

Every family member had to help build the new frontier settlements. Here, a three-year-old girl carries in firewood.

Women miners stayed at camps like this one. To make their crude tents and shacks bearable in freezing weather, they papered the sides with sheets of old newspapers.

hoping to find wealth. And a number of women were among those who sought their fortunes digging for the precious ore.

A miner's camp was full of rough language and actions. It was not considered a proper place for a woman. So if a female prospector wanted to join a camp, she had to disguise herself as a man. But many women were unwilling to do this. Instead, they camped out near their claims with other women miners or by themselves. This way, too, they could better guard their claims.

As time passed, profitable claims became scarce. Even the rich veins of ore quickly drained when tapped, and yielded less and less gold. The average miner worked long hours and made only about three dollars a day. Expenses were extremely high, since food and other supplies had to be brought in from the East. Some people hauled clean water many miles and sold it to the miners for as much as fifty dollars a barrel. A single can of peaches might cost as much as twenty dollars.

Although thousands of people headed for the mining regions, others believed that the new territory between the early frontier settlements and California might be turned into productive farm land. Many thousands of prospectors who failed to find gold or who never reached the gold fields joined the settlers in Nebraska, Utah, the Dakotas, Washington, and Oregon.

Women were active in settling these new areas. Many widowed and single women who hadn't caught "gold fever" were excited about having a farm of their own. Some worked extra hours and saved a part of their earnings for travel expenses. Others formed groups, pooled their few dollars, and headed West. A few women were able to find work as cooks with the wagon trains going West.

A wagon train usually consisted of twenty or more wagons. Because space in the wagons was limited, the settlers could bring few belongings with them. Often a cherished rocking chair or a prized hand-woven quilt had to be left behind. Most wagons only had room for such important items as salt, flour, seeds, and bedding. The entire family slept on a large feather mattress. Cooking utensils and other needed housewares were sometimes hung from the horses' saddles to save wagon space.

Before the journey began, the heads of families met with the wagon master, who was familiar with the route. They drew up regulations to govern the group and insure their safety and to divide chores.

Both female and male family heads signed up to join the wagon trains. The women shared all tasks equally with the men. They did guard duty, patrolling the camp armed with a rifle to ward off animals. They scouted ahead in search of water and to check the trails. And they helped supervise the general progress of the train.

Wagon trains usually left in the spring, before heavy snows could block the mountain passes. But the journey westward was still long and dangerous. Thunderous cloudbursts often flooded the trails. After pushing their wagons through deep mud ditches and over rocks, they still had to swim sizeable streams, dragging their horses and wagons across.

Women family heads were responsible for themselves and their families. When a wagon broke, they repaired it themselves. Often, if a horse died, they hitched themselves up to a wagon to keep going.

Their hands became rough and calloused from driving the teams and doing the repairs. At times, they had to contend with hail storms that tore the canvas tops of their wagons. On other days, they travelled under a scorching sun that burned the leather of their boots. And

Westward-bound pioneers pause for a moment. Often their wagons were so heavily loaded with supplies that there was no room for passengers. Many women walked across the country carrying an infant while leading their older children by the hand.

there was always the danger of disease that might spread if not caught in time. One young girl wrote this account of the hardships she and her family endured:

> In the spring my father decided to go West. My invalid mother protested in vain, she and nine of us children were stowed away in the wagon for six months. But soon my

> mother became victim of that dreaded epidemic, cholera, that struck so many wagon trains that year. After a few days of suffering, she died. We took up our journey again, now too sad to talk, too weary to pray. But ten days later, our Willie, the baby, died. We buried him in the sands of the Burnt River Mountains.

Many died—women, men, children. But most made it to the new frontier.

After arriving on their new land, the families immediately set to work to build a home. This was not an easy task for the land was often bleak and sometimes treeless. Those who chose to settle the grassy plains had no lumber with which to build a log cabin or even a wooden frame for a house.

Instead, these settlers built soddies—homes of dirt

Entire pioneer families lived in small, one-room soddies. There were no indoor toilets or running water. When a woman needed water for washing, cooking or cleaning, she had to walk to the nearest stream and carry back what she could in pails.

and soil. First they plowed up furrows of sod which they molded into foot long blocks. They piled the rows of sod blocks on each other to form walls. Then they covered the one room structure with a thatch roof.

A sod house was warm in the winter and cool in the summer, but families living in them were never really comfortable. Dirt crumbled from the walls, falling on their food and beds. Snakes and gophers often dug tunnels through the walls and floors. And rats and mice lived in the thatch.

Like the early colonial women settlers of the backwoods, frontier women made everything their families needed. Most began work at daybreak and did not rest until late evening. They cooked, spun cloth and made clothing, raised children, and tried to keep their dirt homes clean. They cleared and plowed fields, tended and harvested crops, milked the cows, raised hogs, rode and trained horses, and did just about every chore on the farm.

The women not only worked, they also made most of their own tools. To make pitchforks, they attached handles to deer antlers. Many of the women learned to use a knife well enough to carve spoons, forks, and bowls out of animal bones. They fashioned cups and containers out of vegetable gourds and animal horns.

Pioneer women had to be capable because they were often on their own. Even married women found themselves alone on homesteads much of the time. Twice a

Since there were few trees on the plains, wood was scarce. Women gathered twigs, grass, corncobs, peat, and buffalo chips (manure) to burn as fuel.

year, many of the men travelled long distances to marketing centers to sell the family's crops. This enabled them to get a good price for their produce. But it also kept them away from their families for as long as four months at a time.

Men also went on long hunting expeditions to provide their families with meat and furs for the winter. Still others left their wives to care for the homestead, while they went off in search of better lands to farm.

Many men never returned. Some died fighting Indians whose lands they had invaded. During the 1840s the Plains Indians allowed the pioneers to pass through their hunting grounds. At times, the Indians even guided them, helping them at difficult river crossings. Some tribes supplied the wagon trains with vegetables and buffalo meat in exchange for tobacco, whiskey, and pieces of metal for making different things.

However, in the late 1850s and early 1860s, white farmers began to establish homesteads on Indian lands. To get the Indians to leave the Whites paid them cash for their land. But their money meant nothing to the Indians who didn't realize that if they accepted these slips of paper, they would have to give up their land.

The Indians believed that the land and everything on it was a gift from God to be used fairly by all. They felt that soil, streams, and trees were too precious to be sold. But many Whites believed any piece of property could be bought with enough cash. When they no longer allowed the Indians to hunt in the forests or fish in the streams they had "bought," fierce fighting broke out.

Although most of the fighting was done by men, both Indian and white women suffered greatly. Many lost their husbands and sons in battle. Often when their camps and homesteads were attacked the women were raped, tortured and killed. The fighting lasted for many years.

But even when their men were safe at home, the

Indian women also worked hard. In addition to preparing food and making clothing, they had to care for large families. These are Ute women and children.

women still did much of the work. As small towns with saloons sprang up in the West, some men spent more and more time away from their homesteads. If they remained in town drinking, gambling, trading horses, or taking care of other business, they might not return home for two or three days.

Meanwhile, women saw to it that the homesteads ran smoothly. They handled any emergencies that arose. Most learned to shoot a rifle soon after arriving in the West. Alone so much of the time, they had to protect

Ms. Bertie Lord of Eagle Rock, Montana, killed a coyote that had been raiding pioneer homesteads.

themselves, their children, and their homes against thieves and wild animals.

Coyotes, wolves, bears, and foxes raided their homesteads, killing the farm animals. Pioneer women grabbed their rifles and went with their husbands to hunt down the raiders. When the men weren't around, the women banded together to form their own hunting parties.

In addition to their other duties, frontier housewives often gave food and shelter to travelers. Some of their visitors were men on their way to marketing centers. Others were new settlers who had just come West to search for homesteads. Most prairie towns were very small. There were no hotels or even boarding houses. So travelers simply stopped off at the nearest homestead. One woman described what it was like to run her household as well as attend to her many boarders:

> I, if not washing, scrubbing, churning or nursing the baby, was preparing their meals in our lean-to kitchen. To bear two children in two and a half years from my marriage day, to make thousands of pounds of butter every year for market, not to mention what was used in our free hotel at home. To sew and cook, to wash and iron, to scrub and clean; to be, in short, a general pioneer drudge without a penny of my own, was not pleasant business.

7

☆
☆
☆

Women Against Slavery

☆

MANY WOMEN DID NOT GO WEST. INSTEAD OF TAMING THE frontier, they remained at home to fight other battles. Some became involved in a special crusade for freedom. These women were abolitionists. They believed in freedom for all slaves and were determined to "abolish" or end slavery in the United States.

In the early 1600s, the New World colonists realized that there simply weren't enough hands to do all that was needed. If their settlements were to survive, the colonists would have to solve their labor problems. So they sent to Europe for indentured servants. They paid for their passage, and provided them with food and clothing. In return, the indentured servants served their masters for seven years.

As the colonies continued to grow, so did the need for more workers. By now, most colonists were dissatisfied with indentured servants. They found it too costly to pay for the passage and room and board of a man or woman bound for only seven years. And many indentured servants ran away from the cruelty of their masters or to lead free lives in distant towns.

Then in the 1630s, colonists bought slaves from traders who had bought or kidnapped them from Africa. The colonists did not have to pay slaves for their work, or provide them with decent living or working conditions. And because of their color, it was difficult for black slaves to escape. Many colonists believed they had found an endless source of free labor.

Most slaves in the South did farm work or housework. But there were also slaveowners in New York, New Jersey, Pennsylvania, Delaware and New England. Many of these Northerners taught their slaves to build ships or to become carpenters, mechanics, shoemakers, painters, and seamstresses.

After the American Revolution, most northern states outlawed slavery. But the South still clung to its slaves. These black men, women, and children were very important to the South's economy.

Slaves usually worked for over eighteen hours a day. Often they were given only enough food to survive. Some masters believed it was more profitable to work a young slave to an early death than to care for one in old age. An old slave would no longer be useful in the fields.

A slave who ran away and was caught might be

Women abolitionists helped many slaves find freedom.

severely punished or even killed to prevent others from doing the same. Most slaves believed there were only two ways out of slavery—death or the "underground railroad."

The "underground railroad" was financed and supported by abolitionists.

The underground railroad was not an actual railroad, but a secret route to the North. It ran along backwoods, swamps, and hidden paths in the woods. The "passengers" were runaway slaves, and the "conductors" were abolitionists who helped them on their way. During the daylight hours, the runaways were sheltered in "stations," the homes of abolitionists.

Some of them were Whites who believed slavery was inhumane; others were freed slaves or escaped runaways who wanted to help free other Blacks. Women, both black and white, were especially active in the abolitionist movement.

There were over 3,000 conductors. Among the most heroic was Harriet Tubman. Harriet was a black woman who had escaped from slavery in Maryland without help from anyone. Even before she joined the railroad, she sneaked back again and again to her old plantation until she had freed her entire family. As a runaway slave it was extremely dangerous for Harriet to return to the South at all. But that did not stop her from serving as an underground railroad conductor.

While transporting slaves North, this small slender woman always carried a pistol and spoke with authority. When a slave became frightened and wanted to turn back, she drew out her gun and said, "You go on or you die!" To keep an infant from crying and revealing their whereabouts, she would give the child something to make it sleep. Then she would hide the baby in a burlap sack, which she carefully carried herself.

Many slaves looked to her for their freedom. The white slaveowners feared her and offered a reward of

Tall, slender Isabella Baumfree took the name Sojourner Truth (which means "truthtelling traveler") and journeyed throughout the North to plead for the abolition of slavery.

$40,000 for her capture—dead or alive. But Harriet Tubman was never caught. She rescued over 300 slaves, and never lost a passenger on the railroad to freedom, even though she made the trip South 19 times.

Sojourner Truth was another black woman who fought for her people's freedom. Born into slavery in the state of New York, Sojourner was freed when New York abolished slavery in 1817. As a free woman, she traveled from town to town preaching against slavery. She was a moving speaker as she argued that slavery was cruel and must be outlawed everywhere. She was often insulted, but she continued her crusade.

Once, after hearing her speak, a young male lawyer in the crowd yelled out, "You think your talk does any good, old woman? Why I don't care any more for it than for a fleebite." "Maybe not," she answered with dignity, "but the Lord willing, I'll keep you scratching."

Many white women were active abolitionists as well. They formed groups like the Philadelphia Female Anti-slavery Society. They flooded Congress and state legislatures with letters and petitions against slavery, and held fairs and bazaars to raise funds. They used the money to help newly-freed Blacks, as well as to educate Whites on the evils of slavery.

Sometimes, change came from where it was least expected. The Grimké sisters were the daughters of a large plantation owner from South Carolina. Sarah and Angelina had seen enough of slavery to be violently opposed to it. They spoke out against the cruel system, but realized that they couldn't make any changes so long as they still lived in the South.

The sisters traveled North, where they joined the abolitionist movement. There, Angelina wrote a stirring antislavery appeal to southern women. Her old friends and neighbors became so enraged by the appeal that it was publicly burned. They threatened to imprison Angelina if she ever returned home.

Both sisters went on numerous speaking tours to

persuade people to join the abolitionist's cause. They collected signatures for petitions against slavery. One of Angelina's most successful speaking engagements ended with her presenting an antislavery petition to the Massachusetts state legislature. This marked the first time a woman had ever testified before a legislative committee.

The abolitionists proved to be such excellent persuaders that the South began to regard the antislavery movement as a serious threat to their way of life. Tensions between slaveowners in the South and northern abolitionists increased.

Many Northerners became convinced that slavery should be prohibited in any new state that joined the Union. Southerners protested fiercely against this policy. They knew that if many more states banned slavery than allowed it, abolitionists would soon outnumber slaveholders in voting power, and slavery would be abolished.

Southerners petitioned to the federal government to create an equal number of slave states and free states. But Congress found it impossible to pass laws that satisfied both the North and the South.

Some slaveholders felt the South should withdraw from the Union and form their own nation. But they decided to wait for the results of the 1860 presidential election. The Republican party was controlled by northern abolitionists, while most southern slaveholders were Democrats. The southerners were certain that any Republican president would try to abolish slavery.

The Republican candidate, Abraham Lincoln, won. Eleven southern states left the Union immediately. They elected a slaveowner, Jefferson Davis, as president of their new nation—the Confederate States of America.

Then, on April 12, 1861, Confederate soldiers fired on Fort Sumter, a federal fort in South Carolina. Lincoln realized he would have to use force to protect the nation. And so, the Civil War, or the War Between the States, began.

8

☆
☆
☆

War Between the States

☆

WITH THE OUTBREAK OF FIGHTING, THE NORTH AND THE Confederacy called on their people to join the armed forces. Women answered the call on both sides.

As in the American Revolution, women made bandages, cooked, and laundered for the soldiers. In army hospitals, they established kitchens where they prepared special foods for wounded soldiers. And whether they were trained or untrained, they provided nursing care.

One especially beloved nurse, Mary Ann Bickerdyke, became known as "Mother" to thousands of Union soldiers. Mary cared for "her boys," bringing them warm drinks and medicine even when they were close to the battle lines.

However, Mary could be severe when she had to be. Once she had a ward surgeon dismissed for his repeated drunkness. The man complained to the general.

Many women nursed the sick and wounded during the Civil War. Nurse Clara Barton often drove an oxcart filled with medical supplies to the battle sites. She also trained hundreds of other nurses and later established the American Red Cross.

But when the general learned that Mother Bickerdyke had insisted that the doctor be replaced, he shrugged his shoulders and answered, "I'm sorry, but I can't help you. She outranks me."

On the home fronts of both the North and South, women took the places of men who were now fighting. For the first time, many of them ran businesses and kept up farms and plantations. They supplied the soldiers with food and uniforms, staffed arsenals, and manufactured munitions. In large northern cities, women aided the war effort by handling much of the federal government's paper work. These "government girls" became America's first women clerks and bookkeepers. Such positions had formerly been reserved for men.

Many women wanted to fight in actual combat alongside the men. One day, in April of 1862, some Confederate recruiting officers visited a small Texas town to find volunteers. Only five men signed up. But fifteen young women eagerly stepped forward to join them. However, when the officers realized that the young women were interested in front line fighting, they promptly asked the "ladies" to step back.

But some very determined women—nearly 500 of them—could not be discouraged. They wore men's clothing to take part in the fighting. Frances Cook used the name Frank Miller to enlist in the Union's 19th Illinois Volunteer Regiment. She fought for several months before she was captured. After a week in a southern prison camp, Frances tried to escape, but was shot in the leg. Only while treating her bullet wound, did her captors learn that Frank was really Frances.

However, there were times when both the Union and Confederate armies did use women. As saboteurs, they blew up bridges, cut telephone wires, burned supply houses, and helped war prisoners to escape. Women were very able spies. In fact, a group of teenage girls formed one of the most effective spy rings in the Confederacy!

Women also actively served as scouts and guides. During the course of the war, when President Lincoln freed the slaves, a number of Black women joined the Union's forces. They were outstanding guides, since they had lived in the South most of their lives, and knew the country well.

But perhaps the Black woman who made the greatest contribution to the Union army was Harriet Tubman, the former runaway slave and abolitionist. Harriet organized Black male troops for the Union army and became their commanding officer. On June 2, 1863, she led her soldiers in a raid on Confederate forces. They burned plantations, Confederate warehouses, and arsenals, and set over 500 prisoners-of-war free. She planned and executed the mission so well that not one of her men was killed or even wounded! She became the first woman in America's military history to carry out an attack on enemy forces.

Although Harriet Tubman served bravely during the Civil War, she was never paid. Over 25 years later she was given a small pension because she was a soldier's widow—not because of her own contributions.

9

☆
☆
☆

Feminism Is Born

☆

THE CIVIL WAR ENDED IN 1865 WITH THE NORTH'S VICTORY. When the struggle was over, American women took a long hard look at their status. They didn't like what they saw. They, their mothers, and grandmothers might have worked seven days a week to build the nation. Yet in the 1800s women enjoyed few legal rights.

If a woman married, she lost many liberties granted to men and single women by law. She could not legally own property. Even if she inherited property before she married, it belonged to her husband as of their wedding day.

When a married woman was employed outside her home, her salary legally belonged to her husband. If he wished, he could collect her wages and spend it all without giving her a cent.

If a woman left home, she lost everything. The

house, the furnishings, even her jewelry were considered her husband's property. The children remained with their father. The woman was legally stopped from taking them along with her. She couldn't change the laws by electing government officials who favored the cause of women. Women didn't even have the right to vote!

The seeds of the Women's Rights Movement actually began to take root before the Civil War. Dissatisfied with their position, women banded together to work for change. In 1848, they held the first Women's Rights Convention in the small New York town of Seneca Falls.

A woman named Elizabeth Cady Stanton put one small notice of the convention in a local newspaper, and

Women's Rights leader, Elizabeth Cady Stanton, holds her daughter Harriot. Over a quarter of a century later, Harriot took up her mother's unfinished crusade and became a suffragette herself.

over 300 women flocked to this "public meeting for protest and discussion." They came from as far as 100 miles away in wagons, on horseback, even on foot. And they issued the following statement:

> We hold these truths to be self-evident: that all men and women are created equal.

At the meeting, Elizabeth Cady Stanton declared, "It is the sacred duty of women to secure the elective franchise." The others agreed, and they demanded the right to vote.

During the next few years, women continued to work for equality. However, when the Civil War broke out, they turned to saving their country. But after the war, feelings for the Women's Rights Movement stirred once again.

Pioneer women who had waged a successful battle with the rugged frontier were now ready to fight for equality. Northern women who had worked to abolish slavery looked forward to working for their own liberation.

Black women, freed from slavery, hoped to also find freedom as women. Sojourner Truth now addressed herself to the woman question. Once while attending a Women's Rights, or Feminist, public gathering, she heard a group of men scoff at the idea of giving the vote to women. The men claimed that women were helpless creatures who had to be helped into carriages and carried over mud puddles. To answer them, Sojourner raised her right arm and said:

> Look at my arm! I have ploughed and planted and gathered into barns . . . and ain't I a woman? I could work as much and eat as much as any man—when I could get it—and bear the lash as well . . . I have borne thirteen children and seen most of them sold off into slavery, and when I cried out with my mother's grief, none but Jesus helped me—and ain't I a woman?

Over the years, many other women who fought for the vote learned to respond with equal fire to taunting remarks. Called suffragettes, they staged marches, circulated petitions, sent speakers to all parts of the country, and urged elected officials to change unjust laws.

As time passed, the Feminists became convinced that they would have to stage a daring event to forcefully protest their lack of rights. One of their leaders, Susan B. Anthony, thought of a suffrage protest that made history. The idea came to her while she was reading a newspaper article reminding men to vote in an upcoming election. "If you were not permitted to vote," it said, "you would fight for the right . . . die for it."

Susan B. Anthony, whose energy and drive inspired countless other women, argued that a woman did not need a husband to enjoy a full life, and so she never married.

"Absolutely correct," thought Susan. And on election day in November of 1872, she, along with fifteen other Feminists, arrived at the polls in Rochester, New York. They proudly cast their ballots. It was the first time women had ever voted in a federal election!

The women were allowed to leave the polls without incident. But later, on November 28, Thanksgiving Day, the police came to their homes and charged them with violating a federal act. They were promptly hauled off to jail. The charges against everyone except Susan were eventually dropped. But Susan B. Anthony was charged by a grand jury for "knowingly, wrongfully, and unlawfully voting for a representative in the Congress of the United States."

Susan was forbidden to speak during her trial. The male judge claimed that she was not "competent" to testify "as a witness in her own behalf." Susan B. Anthony was found guilty. But when the judge asked, "Has the prisoner anything to say before sentence is pronounced?", she replied:

> Yes, your Honor, I have many things to say. For in your verdict of guilty, you have trampled underfoot every vital principle of our government. My natural rights, my civil rights, my political rights, my judicial rights, are all alike ignored. Robbed of the fundamental principle of citizenship, I (and) . . .

> all my sex are, by your Honor's verdict, doomed to political subjugation under this so called form of government.

The judge ordered her to pay a $100 fine. But she refused saying, "May it please your Honor, I shall never pay a dollar of your unjust penalty." The fine was never collected.

In time, the Feminist movement had some success. By the turn of the nineteenth century, a few of the most unfair marriage and divorce laws had been changed. More women began attending college. Mount Holyoke, the first college for women, was established. And Smith and Vassar, two other fine colleges for women, soon followed.

The Women's Rights Movement proved to American women that they were entitled to pursue any career, as well as vote. Soon, they demanded entrance to professions that before were for men only. One such woman was Lucy Hobbs Taylor.

When she was twenty-six, Lucy decided to become a dentist. In 1859, there were no women dentists in America, but that did not stop Lucy. At that time, dentists learned their trade by either attending college or becoming an apprentice. Lucy wanted to go to a university, but no school would accept her because she was a woman.

When she tried to find a dentist whom she could

study under as an apprentice, Lucy met more obstacles. Many dentists were shocked by the idea of a woman dentist. They told Lucy that she was "foolish" and that "a decent woman should remain at home." One dentist said he would allow her to clean his office and watch him work—if she promised not to tell anyone that she was learning dentistry.

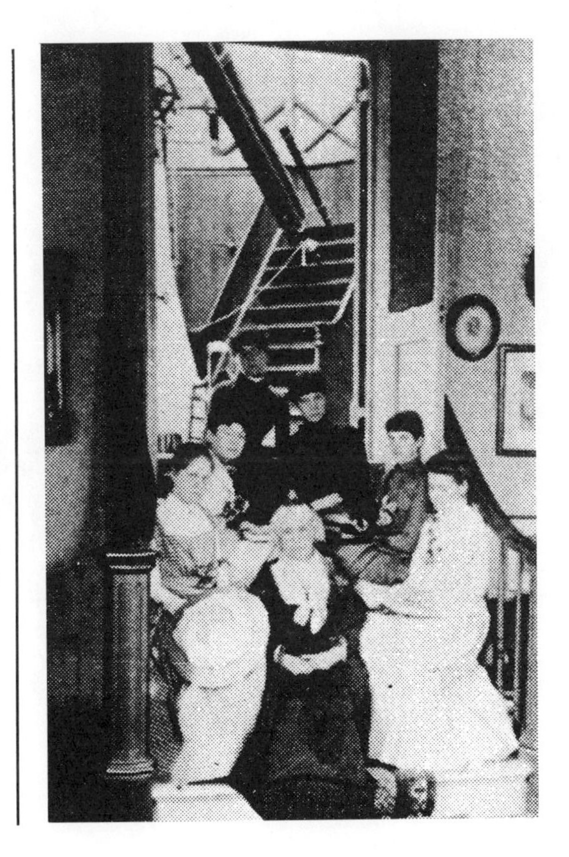

Astronomer Maria Mitchell discovered a comet which was later named for her. In 1850, she became the first woman to be elected to the distinguished scientific society, The American Academy of Arts and Sciences.

A class of women medical school students dissect cadavers at the Women's Medical College of Pennsylvania. Elizabeth Blackwell, the first woman to attend medical school, graduated in 1849 at the top of her class.

But Lucy Hobbs Taylor continued her search for a dentist to study under. And after three years, she found one.

Lucy was an outstanding student. When she entered some samples of her work in a dentistry exhibition she won first prize, even though she was an apprentice competing with already established dentists. Hoping the contest might influence the colleges that had rejected her, Lucy reapplied. But the schools still refused to admit her.

After her apprenticeship, Lucy began to practice dentistry. She soon earned an excellent reputation. Both men and women traveled many miles by stagecoach to be treated by "the highly skilled lady dentist." Once again, Lucy Hobbs Taylor applied to dentistry school. Although she was already a successful dentist, she claimed, "that there was still much more to learn."

Finally, she was admitted to Ohio College of Dental Surgery. She graduated in November 1865, the only woman in a class of eighteen men. And for the first time in history, the degree of Doctor of Dental Surgery was granted to a woman.

Other women made gains like this, too. As a young girl, Louise Bethune was said to have "shown great promise in planning houses and various other structures." As an adult, she was determined to become America's first woman architect.

Louise knew that most young architects learned their skills by working in the drafting rooms of professional architects. Although most architects did not want to employ a woman, she convinced a fairly well-known architect to give her a chance.

Louise worked from six in the morning to six in the evening. She didn't receive much pay, but she learned as she worked, and her employer allowed her to use his large library.

In 1881, after five years of work and study, Louise Bethune felt she was ready to go off on her own. She rented an office and put an ad in a local newspaper stating that "the first professional woman architect in the country was ready for business."

Louise did very well. She insisted that she would not be limited to designing private homes because she was a woman. Instead, she sought out a variety of jobs. Louise Bethune built chapels, storage buildings, factories, and schools. She inspired other women to become architects, and argued that women in the profession should be treated fairly. She often spoke out for "equal pay for equal service."

American women continued to invade new areas of employment. Sarah G. Bagley became America's first woman telegrapher. Rebecca Pennell Dean became the first woman college professor in the United States, and Belva Ann Lockwood the first woman lawyer to practice before the U.S. Supreme Court.

Women made many valuable contributions to America's advancement. But even after proving their ability in almost every profession, they were still considered incapable of voting intelligently. They were denied the ballot.

At the age of 85, when Susan B. Anthony was questioned about women's lack of success in gaining the vote, she answered, "I have never lost my faith. Not for a moment. Failure is impossible." Yet at the time of her death in 1906, only four states had granted women suffrage.

10

☆
☆
☆

The Power to Rock the Nation

☆

THE STRUGGLE FOR SUFFRAGE CONTINUED AFTER SUSAN B. Anthony's death. New leaders arose to carry on the crusade. Carrie Chapman Catt, a school administrator, and Harriot Blatch, Elizabeth Cady Stanton's daughter, were among the group.

In 1913, Woodrow Wilson was elected president of the United States. The Feminists were especially anxious to make their position clear to him. So, on the day before he was to take the inaugural oath, over 5,000 Feminists arrived in Washington, D.C. to stage a protest march through the capital. President-elect Wilson arrived at a nearly empty Washington railroad station that day. But crowds thronged the women's parade route.

By 1900, over 20% of all American women worked outside the home. They were very active in the struggle for labor reform and protested for better wages, shorter working hours, and accident protection.

News of the incident was quickly reported in newspapers across the country. The Feminists had captured the nation's attention! And they were determined to keep it.

They decided to picket the White House. Every day for a year, well dressed women, carrying banners bearing Feminist slogans, paraded in front of the presidential residence. They marched in shifts so there would always be women reminding the White House of their presence.

But the women were not always allowed to picket peacefully. Their opponents often used unlawful and violent tactics. The pickets were attacked by mobs of hoodlums, by uniformed soldiers and sailors, by government clerks, and even the police. They threw raw eggs at the women and tore their clothing. They even burned the women's arms with cigar butts, and dragged some of them by the hair through the streets.

Despite such abuse, the Feminists continued their daily protest. To get the pickets out of the White House area and the public eye, police began to arrest the women. They claimed the women were blocking traffic. But photographs taken of the pickets proved they were not in the street, but against the White House fence.

At first, the public appeared not to care about the Feminists' trouble. At one point, President Wilson even wrote a letter to his daughter in which he stated that the suffragettes "seemed bent on making their cause as obnoxious as possible."

Obnoxious means disagreeable, but that better described the conditions endured by the Feminists who were put in jail. Not only were they unlawfully jailed for long periods of time, they were also kept in damp, overcrowded cells. There were worms in their food, and they were given water in pails used by all the prisoners, both sick and healthy. Some of the prisoners were repeatedly beaten. One 73-year-old suffragette died of a heart attack after being dragged down an iron staircase.

To protest against such horrors, many of the jailed Feminists refused food. Their hunger strikes embarassed the police who denied that the women were mistreated. To make sure none of the Feminists died of starvation, they fed the women by force. Sometimes it took as many as five policemen to hold down one of the women during these "meals."

Still, the suffragettes continued to protest. They knew they were right, and this knowledge gave them courage.

Gradually, public opinion began to go in their favor. Women had helped to build the colonies, settle the frontier, and defend their country. By now, most Americans were convinced that women should have the right to vote. Finally, on August 26, 1920, Congress passed the 19th Amendment, granting all American women suffrage.

The predictions of Feminist leader, Susan B. Anthony, made over half a century ago had come true at last. For these women, "Failure had been impossible." Those who had long rocked the cradle, had finally won the power to rock the nation!

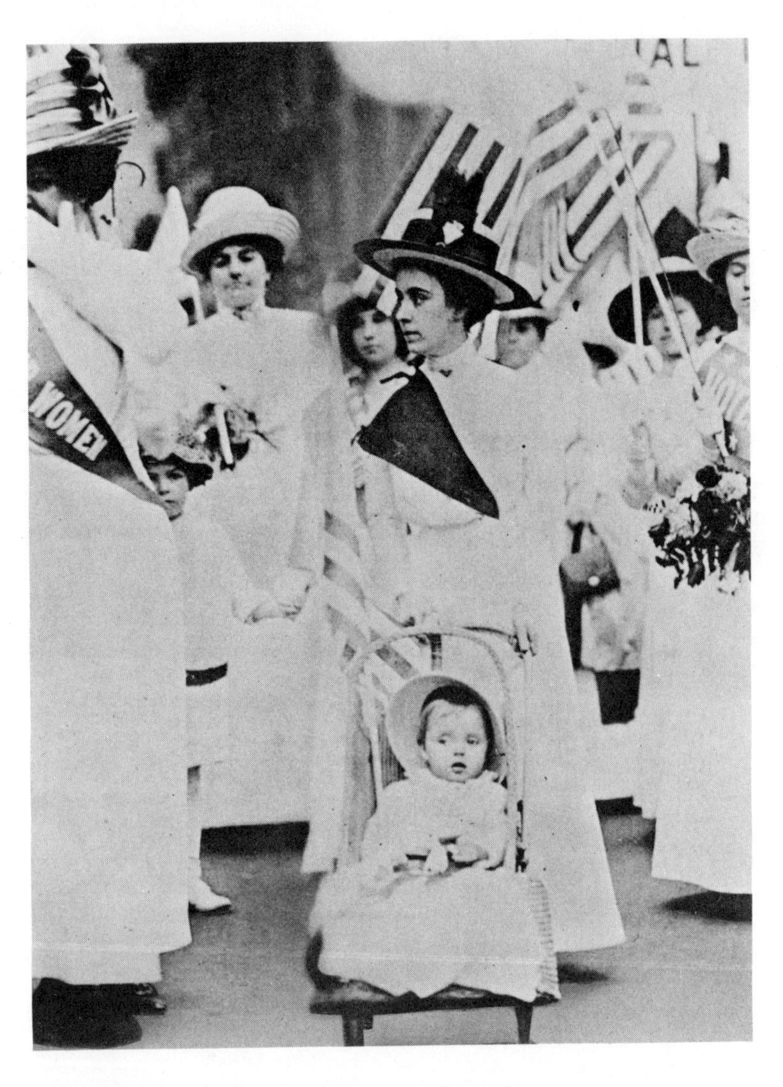

Women of all ages and races marched in suffrage parades.

Some Other Hidden Heroines*

Adams, Abigail, patriot
Addams, Jane, settlement worker
Alcott, Louisa May, author

Barnett, Ida Wells, journalist
Barton, Clara, nurse
Beecher, Catherine, educator
Blakeway, Sarah, colonial planter
Bloomer, Amelia, social and dress reformer
Bowker, Katharine, colonial businesswoman
Boyd, Belle, Confederate spy
Bradstreet, Anne, colonial poet
Brown, Antoinette, minister

Callahan, Mary, colonial midwife
Cary, Mary Ann, abolitionist
Cashman, Nellie, miner and labor arbitrator
Cassatt, Mary, painter
Cheer, Margaret, colonial actress
Child, Lydia Maria, novelist
Corbin, Margaret, Revolutionary War soldier
Cushman, Pauline, Union army spy

Derricotte, Juliette, social worker and humanitarian
Dickinson, Emily, poet
Dix, Dorothea Lynde, pioneer in mental health reform
Drayton, Ann, colonial planter
Drew, Louisiana Lane, actress and stage director
Duncan, Isadora, dancer
Dyer, Mary, religious dissenter

Forrester, Anne, colonial businesswoman
Foster, Abby Kelly, abolitionist
Foster, Hannah, author
Fuller, Margaret, literary critic

Glover, Elizabeth, printer and publisher
Green, Anne Catherine, colonial publisher
Greenhow, Rose O'Neal, Confederate spy

*These women lived during the same period of this book, but are not mentioned in the text.

Hale, Sarah Josepha, writer and editor
Hallam, Sarah, colonial actress
Hayden, Sophia G., architect
Hebden, Katharine, colonial physician
Heck, Barbara, religious leader
Hosmer, Harriet, artist
Howe, Julia Ward, song writer and suffragette
Hoyland, Anna Maria, colonial educator
Hutchinson, Anne, religious dissenter

Inch, Jane, colonial silversmith

Jones, Mary Harris, labor leader
Johnson, Mary, colonial pharmacist

Kelso, Tessa, librarian

Lease, Mary Elizabeth, political leader
Lee, Ann, religious leader
Lee, Mary Ann, ballerina
Lewis, Edmonia, sculptor
Logan, Martha, colonial horticulturist
Lyon, Mary, educator

Massey, Jane, colonial gunsmith
Moody, Deborah, colony founder
Moore, Anne, colonial inn proprietor
Morris, Esther, pioneer suffragette
Mott, Lucretia, abolitionist and women's rights activist

Nation, Carry, temperance crusader
Nuthead, Dianah, colonial printer

Peabody, Elizabeth, educator, writer, lecturer

Richards, Ellen H., chemist
Roberts, Mary, colonial artist
Russell, Elizabeth, colonial shipwright

Sacajawea, explorer and guide
Sanger, Margaret, pioneer in the field of birth control
Seaman, Elizabeth Cochrane, reporter who wrote under the name of Nellie Bly
Sinclair, Elizabeth, colonial inn proprietor
Smith, Erminnie A., geologist
Stagg, Mary, colonial actress
Stephens, Ann S., author
Stewart, Maria W., abolitionist
Stowe, Lucy, women's rights activist

Storer, Maria, colonial actress
Stowe, Harriet Beecher, antislavery writer
Swisshelm, Jane, journalist

Taylor, Nellie, governor
Timothy, Elizabeth, colonial publisher

Van Lew, Elizabeth, Union spy

Wald, Lillian, public health worker
Walker, Maggie Mitchell, banker
Ward, Nancy, a leader of the Cherokee tribes during Revolutionary War
Warden, Margaret, colonial businesswoman
Warren, Mercy Otis, political satirist
Weaver, Lucy, colonial businesswoman
Wentworth, Sarah, novelist
Weyman, Rebecca, colonial upholsterer
Wheatley, Julia, colonial pharmacist
Wheatley, Phillis, poet
Wilkinson, Jemina, religious leader
Willard, Emma Hart, educator
Willard, Frances, temperance crusader
Woodhull, Victoria C., stockbroker

Yates, Elizabeth, colonial planter

Zenger, Catherine, publisher

Index

K

L

M

N

O

P

W